THE ULTIMATE
Owls
BOOK FOR KIDS

Copyright © 2026 by Jenny Kellett

Owls: The Ultimate Book for Kids
www.bellanovabooks.com

All rights reserved. No part of this book may be reproduced in any form by any electronic or mechanical means including photocopying, recording, or information storage and retrieval without permission in writing from the author.
HARDCOVER
Imprint: Bellanova Books
ISBN: 9786192641528

CONTENTS

Introduction 4
Owl Species 8
Typical Owls: *Strigidae* 9
Barn Owls: *Tytonidae* 16
Owl Anatomy 21
Owls in Action 31
Owl Talk 34
Owls: Masters of disguise 38
Breeding & reproduction 45
Conservation & Threats 55
What can you do to help? 58
Owls & The Ecosystem 60
More Owl Fun Facts 64
The Owl Quiz 84
Answers 88
Word search 90
Solution 92
Sources 93

INTRODUCTION

Hey there, owl lover! Ready to discover what makes owls some of the most amazing birds on Earth? Before we dive in, let's take a quick look at some of the key things you need to know about owls.

What are owls?

Owls belong to a group of birds called **raptors**, also known as **birds of prey**. There are over 200 different species of owls living on every continent except Antarctica. Some are big, some are tiny, and they come in all kinds of colors and patterns. No two owls are exactly alike!

Incredible Night Vision

Owls have large, forward-facing eyes that help them see extremely well in the dark. Their eyes are packed with special cells called **rods**, which are perfect for low-light vision. This means an owl can spot a small animal from more than 100 feet (30 meters) away — even in near-total darkness!

Silent Hunters

Owls are some of the quietest flyers in the world. Their feathers are specially shaped to soften the sound of air moving over their wings. This lets them glide through the night and surprise their prey without making a single noise. It's like they have built-in stealth mode!

A Flexible Neck for a Better View

You may have heard that owls can turn their heads all the way around — but that isn't quite true. They can't spin 360 degrees, but they can turn their heads about 270 degrees. That gives them a huge field of view without needing to move their whole body.

Superior Hearing

Owls also have incredible hearing. Their ears are placed slightly unevenly on their heads, which helps them tell exactly where a sound is coming from. This allows them to locate tiny animals, even if they're hidden under leaves or snow — like having their own built-in GPS.

Now that you've met these fascinating nighttime hunters, it's time to go deeper.

In this book, you'll learn about different owl species, where they live, how they hunt, and much more. At the end, you can even test yourself in the owl quiz. **Are you ready?! Let's go!**

OWL SPECIES
A world of owls

Let's explore the fantastic range of owl species found across the globe.

Owls belong to two main families: **Strigidae**, or "true owls," and **Tytonidae**, or "barn owls." Each family has its own unique traits, but both are equally fascinating.

TRUE OWLS:
STRIGIDAE

The Strigidae family is the larger of the two families of owls, with over 200 different species. These owls, known as true owls, are what most people think of when they imagine an owl.

Let's meet some of the most well-known Strigidae owls!

Great Horned Owl

With their tall feather "horns" and bright yellow eyes, great horned owls are some of the most recognizable owls in the world. They live all across North and South America and can be found in forests, deserts, swamps, and even cities. These tough birds are excellent hunters that eat everything from mice and rabbits to birds and insects.

The great horned owl's scientific name is *Bubo virginianus*. Its "horns" are actually ear tufts made of feathers, not real ears, and they may help with camouflage or communication. These owls also have amazing night vision, which helps them spot prey in the dark from far away.

DID YOU KNOW?

Great horned owls are very territorial. They use their deep, booming hoots to warn other owls to stay away and to mark their territory.

Snowy Owl

These beautiful owls have stunning white feathers and bright yellow eyes. They live in the chilly Arctic and are great at staying warm thanks to their thick, cozy feathers. Unlike other owls, they often hunt during the day, especially when Arctic nights are short.

Snowy owls (scientific name: *Bubo scandiacus*) change their feather colors to match changes in their environment throughout the year, going from bright white in winter to a mix of white and black markings in summer!

Burrowing Owl

The burrowing owl (scientific name: *Athene cunicularia*), also called the shoco, is a small, long-legged owl that prefers life on the ground. Found in North and South America, they live in open grasslands and prairies, nesting in abandoned burrows of other animals, such as prairie dogs.

Burrowing owls also have some unique tricks up their feathers. To keep their burrows safe from predators, they scatter animal dung around the entrance. This attracts tasty insects, making it a perfect snack spot for the owls while they guard their home.

BARN OWLS
TYTONIDAE

The Tytonidae family is made up of around 20 species, including the well-known **barn owl**.

These owls have heart-shaped facial discs and dark, beady eyes.

Let's take a closer look at some of the most common Tytonidae species.

Masked Owl

Known for their striking facial patterns, masked owls (scientific name: *tyto novaehollandiae*) are native to Australia and New Guinea. These secretive birds live in dense forests, where they hunt at night for a variety of prey, including possums and tree-dwelling mammals.

©JJ Harrison

Barn Owl

Meet the barn owl (scientific name: *tyto alba*), a truly amazing bird that can be found on every continent except for Antarctica.

These owls have a unique, heart-shaped face and large, dark eyes that make them look like they're wearing a mask.

Unlike most owls, barn owls don't have one ear higher than the other. However, their excellent hearing abilities are still used to pinpoint the exact location of their prey through their unique heart-shaped facial disc that captures and directs sound waves towards their ears.

Most owls are known for their distinctive hooting calls, but barn owls are different. They emit a loud, eerie screech that can be both startling and fascinating.

And you can probably guess where they get their name from. Yes, they love to nest in manmade structures, including in barns!

OWL ANATOMY

How Owls Are Built for the Night

In this chapter, we'll explore the remarkable anatomy (body parts) that makes owls perfectly adapted to their nocturnal lives. From their great eyesight to their silent flight, owls are truly built for the night.

Eyes That See in the Dark

One of the most amazing things about owls is their big, forward-facing eyes. These eyes are specially built for seeing at night and help owls spot even the tiniest movement in the dark.

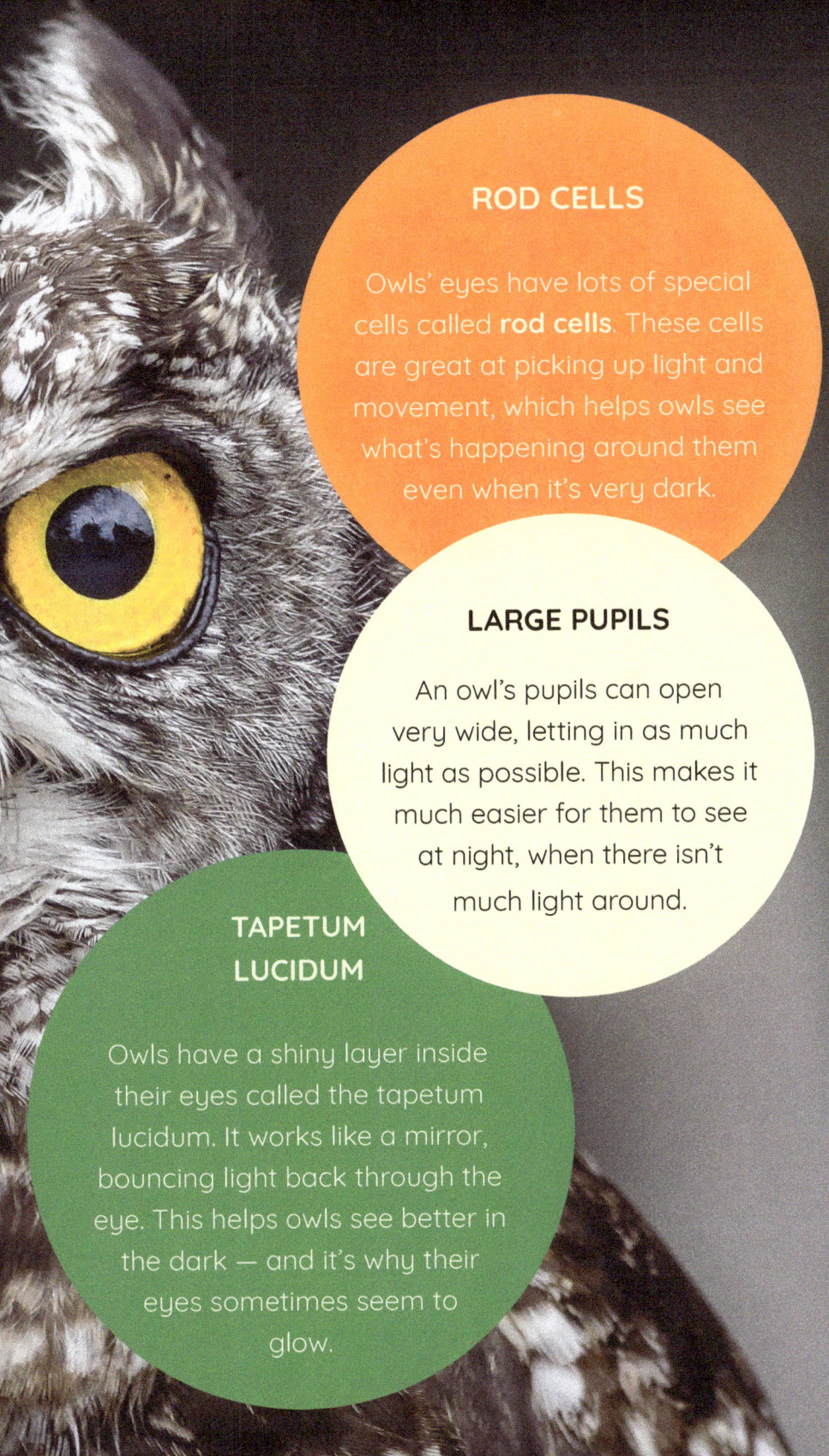

ROD CELLS

Owls' eyes have lots of special cells called **rod cells**. These cells are great at picking up light and movement, which helps owls see what's happening around them even when it's very dark.

LARGE PUPILS

An owl's pupils can open very wide, letting in as much light as possible. This makes it much easier for them to see at night, when there isn't much light around.

TAPETUM LUCIDUM

Owls have a shiny layer inside their eyes called the tapetum lucidum. It works like a mirror, bouncing light back through the eye. This helps owls see better in the dark — and it's why their eyes sometimes seem to glow.

Hearing that finds prey

Owls have amazing hearing that helps them find animals even in complete darkness. Their ears and the special feathers on their faces work together to tell them exactly where a sound is coming from.

ASYMMETRICAL EARS

Many owls have ears that are not in the same place on both sides of their head — one is slightly higher than the other. This helps them tell whether a sound is coming from above, below, left, or right, so they can find their prey with incredible accuracy.

FACIAL DISCS

The feathers around an owl's eyes form a round shape called a facial disc. This works like a sound catcher, guiding noises straight toward the owl's ears so it can hear even the quietest movements.

A long-eared owl (*asio otus*).

The Art of SIlent Flight

If you're an owl, being quiet is very important — you don't want your prey to hear you coming!

Luckily, owls have special feathers that help them fly through the air almost silently.

SOFT FEATHER EDGES

The edges of an owl's wing feathers are not smooth. They are slightly jagged, which helps break up the air as it moves past the wings and makes much less noise.

VELVETY SURFACE

Owls' feathers feel soft and velvety. This texture helps soak up sound, so the air moving over their wings doesn't make loud whooshing noises.

FEATHER FRINGES

Some owls have tiny comb-like fringes along the front edge of their wings. These help control the airflow and make their flight even quieter.

Flexible necks for better vision

Owls have very flexible necks that let them turn their heads about 270 degrees. That means they can look far to the side or even almost behind them without moving their bodies — perfect for spotting prey. They can do this because of some amazing body features:

MORE NECK BONES
Owls have 14 neck bones, while humans only have 7. Having more bones in their neck gives them extra flexibility so they can twist and turn much more than we can.

SPECIAL BLOOD VESSELS
Owls also have special blood vessels that keep blood flowing to their brain when they turn their heads. This stops their blood supply from being cut off, even when their neck is twisted, so their brains always get the oxygen they need.

A barn owl with its prey—a vole.

OWLS IN ACTION

The amazing hunting techniques of owls

Owls are famous for being incredible hunters. These nighttime birds have special skills that help them sneak up on prey and catch it quickly.

Let's take a closer look at how they do it!

Surprise!

Owls are experts at sneaking up on their prey. They often sit quietly on a high branch, watching and listening for movement below. When they spot an animal, they swoop down in one smooth, fast flight and grab it with their powerful talons before it has time to escape.

A brown wood owl.

Versatile Predators

Owls can hunt many different kinds of animals, from tiny insects to birds and small mammals. What an owl eats depends on where it lives and how big it is. For example, the **burrowing owl** often hunts insects and small creatures on the ground, while the **snowy owl** hunts during the daytime in the Arctic when the sun never sets.

Swooping and snatching

When an owl finds its target, it dives down from a branch or glides over the ground. Using its sharp claws, it quickly grabs its prey and holds on tightly. Owls have very strong feet, which helps make sure their meal doesn't get away.

THE ULTIMATE OWL BOOK

OWL TALK

How Owls Communicate

Owls use lots of different sounds to talk to each other. These calls help them stay safe, find a mate, and take care of their families.

Let's listen in and find out what owls are really saying!

A ferruginous pygmy owl.

Hoots and Calls

One of the most famous owl sounds is the hoot. Different owl species have different hoots, so people who study owls can tell them apart just by listening.

Owls use hoots for several reasons:

TERRITORY
Owls hoot to tell other owls, "This area is taken!"

MATING
During breeding season, owls hoot to attract a partner and stay in touch with their mate.

COMMUNICATION
Owls also use hoots to talk to nearby family members or neighbors.

Besides hooting, owls can screech, whistle, chirp, or hiss. These sounds can be used to warn of danger or scare away threats.

The Quiet Hunting Call

When owls are hunting, they sometimes use soft, high-pitched calls to communicate with their partner. These quiet sounds are hard for humans to hear and help owls work together without giving away their position.

Baby Owl Sounds: Begging for Food

Baby owls, called owlets, make lots of noise when they're hungry! They use high-pitched, raspy calls to tell their parents it's time to eat. This "begging call" helps make sure they get enough food to grow big and strong.

Listening to Owls in the Wild

If you ever hear strange sounds outside at night, it might be owls talking to each other. Listening for owls can be fun, and there are even apps that can help you figure out which owl you're hearing just by its call.

MASTERS OF DISGUISE

Owls are amazing at hiding in their surroundings. Using their feathers, colors, and clever behavior, they can blend into trees, leaves, snow, and shadows so well that they're almost invisible.

Let's see how they do it!

A great grey owl.

FANCY FEATHERS

Owls have special feathers that help them stay hidden. Their colors and patterns often match the places where they live, making it hard for other animals to spot them.

Bark-like Patterns

Some owls, like the **eastern screech owl** (*below*), have feathers that look just like tree bark. When they sit on a tree trunk or branch, they can be almost impossible to see.

Photo by Greg Hume

Leafy Greens

Some owls like the **long-eared owl** (*left*) have brown and greenish feathers that look like leaves and twigs. This helps them blend into bushes and trees.

Snow White

The **snowy owl** (*right*) has white feathers that help it disappear into the snowy Arctic landscape.

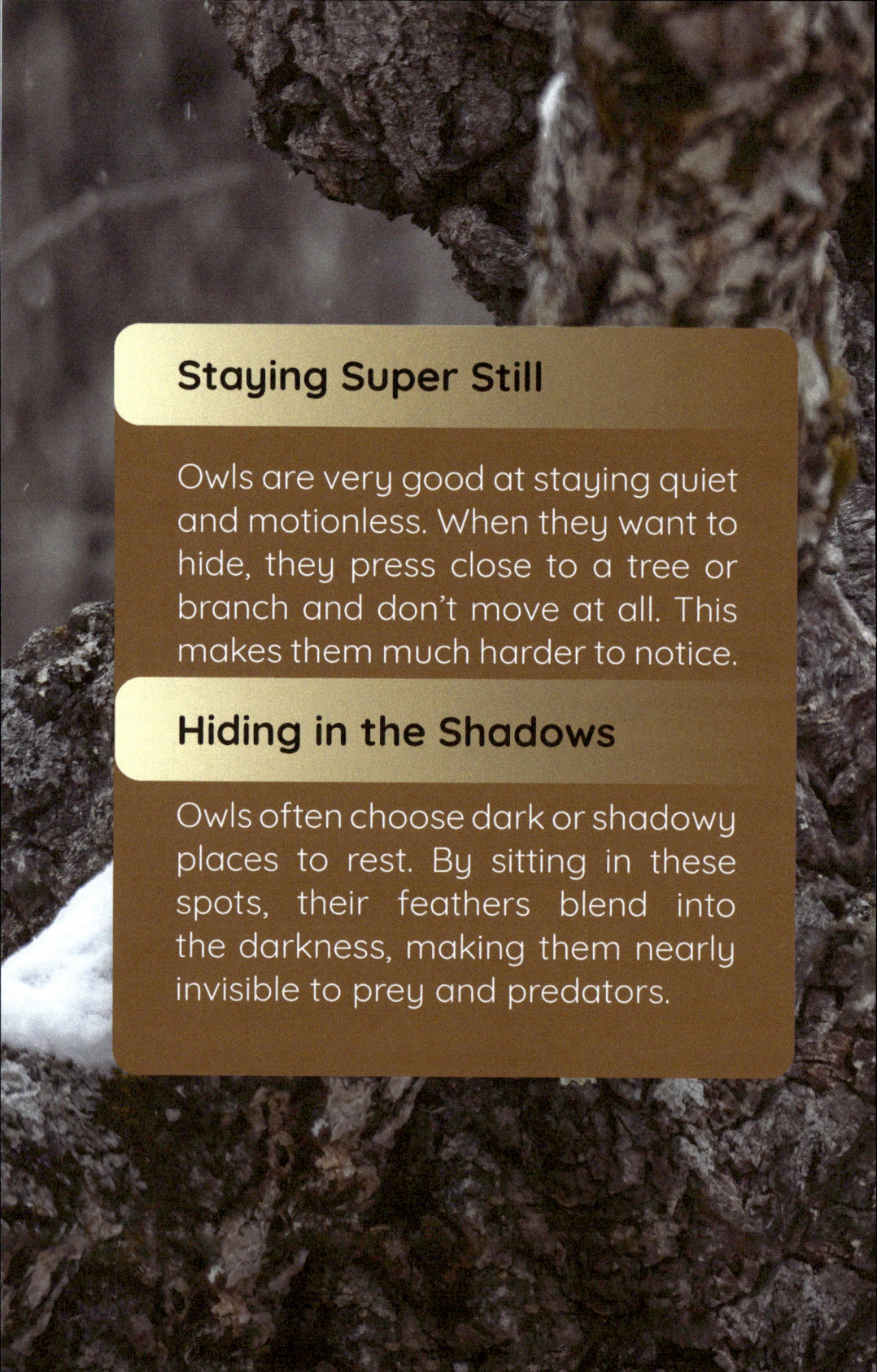

Staying Super Still

Owls are very good at staying quiet and motionless. When they want to hide, they press close to a tree or branch and don't move at all. This makes them much harder to notice.

Hiding in the Shadows

Owls often choose dark or shadowy places to rest. By sitting in these spots, their feathers blend into the darkness, making them nearly invisible to prey and predators.

Clever Nesting Spots

Owls choose nesting places that help keep them and their babies safe. Some nest inside hollow trees, while others use old nests made by other birds. By picking hidden, sheltered spots, owls protect their eggs and young from danger.

BREEDING & REPRODUCTION

Baby animals are always cute — and owls are no exception! Let's explore how baby owls, called owlets, grow from tiny eggs into strong, flying hunters.

From hatching to leaving home, owlets go on an amazing journey as they learn how to survive in the wild.

EGGS

An owl's life starts inside an egg. Mother owls lay their eggs in safe places, like hollow trees or old nests left behind by other birds.

The number of eggs depends on the species — some owls lay just one, while others can lay several. While the eggs are growing, one or both parents keep them warm and protected.

HATCHING

After a few weeks, the eggs are ready to hatch. The baby owls use a tiny, sharp bump called an **egg tooth** to crack open the shell. With a lot of wiggling and pushing, the owlets break free and enter the world.

NESTLINGS

Once they hatch, baby owls are called nestlings. They are covered in soft, fluffy feathers called **down** and depend completely on their parents for food and safety. The parents bring food to the nest many times a day to feed their hungry chicks.

As they grow, their fluffy down is replaced by stronger feathers. They also start stretching their wings and practicing their balance.

BRANCHING

As the owlets get bigger, they begin a stage called **branching**. They leave the nest and start climbing or hopping onto nearby branches. This helps them explore their surroundings and build strength, even though they still return to their parents for food and care.

FLEDGING

Next comes **fledging**, when young owls start learning to fly. At first, it can be a little wobbly as they practice taking off and landing. Their parents continue to watch over them and bring food while they improve their flying skills.

INDEPENDENCE: READY FOR THE WILD

When the young owls can fly well and hunt on their own, they are ready to leave home. They move away to find their own territory and begin life as adult owls.

DID YOU KNOW?

Around 30% of owl species worldwide are currently at risk of extinction.

CONSERVATION & THREATS

Owls are strong and clever birds, but they still need our help. Many things people do can make life harder for owls, like cutting down forests or using harmful chemicals.

The good news is that when we understand these dangers, we can also learn how to protect owls and keep them safe.

Habitat Loss

One of the biggest problems for owls is losing their homes. When forests, fields, and old trees are cleared to build roads, farms, or houses, owls lose the places where they hunt and nest. Without enough safe places to live, it becomes harder for owls to find food and raise their babies.

Climate Change

Climate change is changing the weather all over the world. Some places are getting hotter, colder, or drier than before. This can affect the animals that owls eat and the places where they live. When food becomes harder to find, owls must work much harder just to survive.

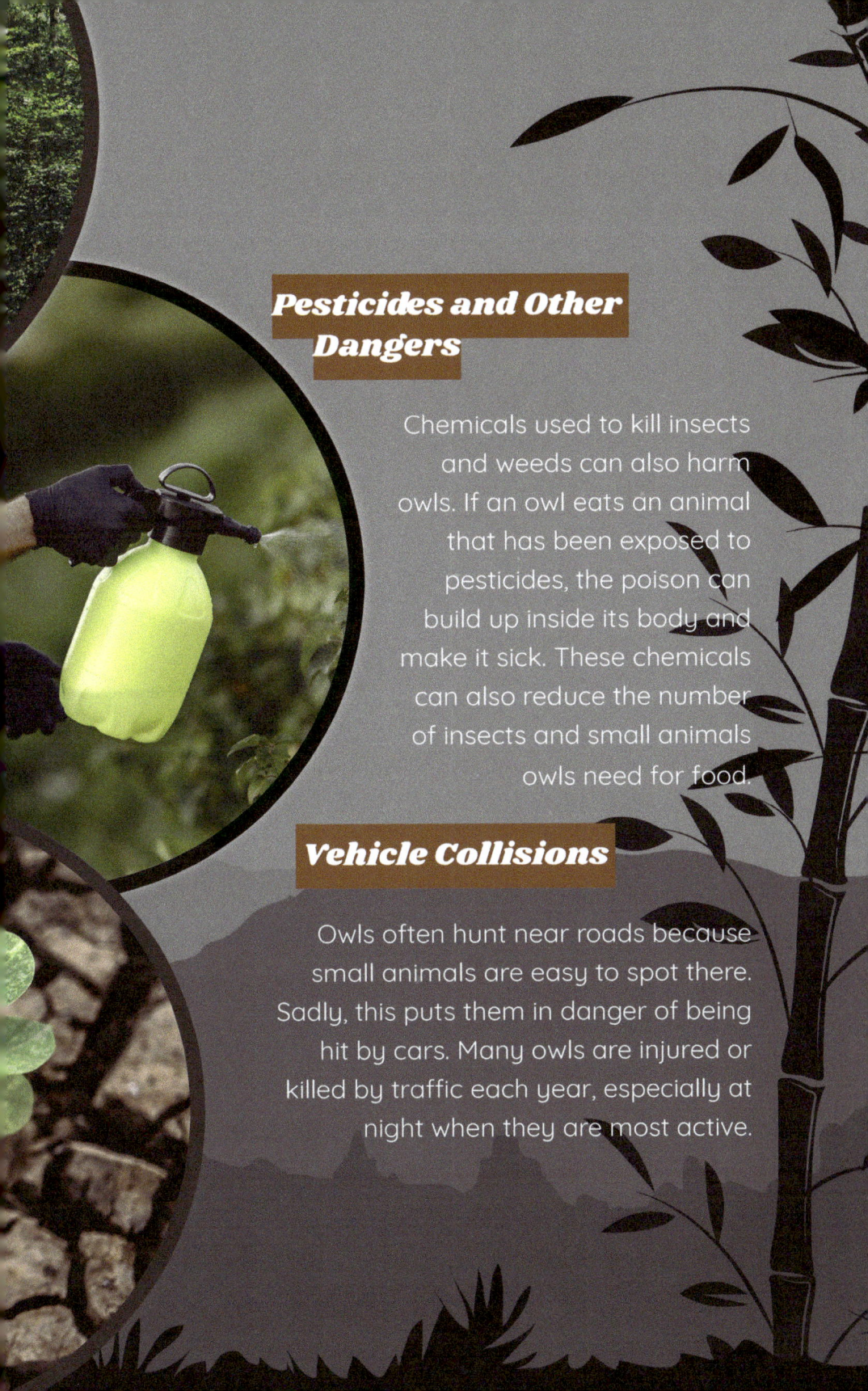

Pesticides and Other Dangers

Chemicals used to kill insects and weeds can also harm owls. If an owl eats an animal that has been exposed to pesticides, the poison can build up inside its body and make it sick. These chemicals can also reduce the number of insects and small animals owls need for food.

Vehicle Collisions

Owls often hunt near roads because small animals are easy to spot there. Sadly, this puts them in danger of being hit by cars. Many owls are injured or killed by traffic each year, especially at night when they are most active.

WHAT CAN YOU DO TO HELP?

Everyone can help make the world a safer place for owls. Even small actions can make a big difference! Here are some simple ways you can help protect owls and become a true Owl Hero.

Create a Wildlife-Friendly Yard

You can help owls right at home! Plant native trees and bushes, put up birdhouses or owl nest boxes, and avoid using harmful chemicals in your garden. These things create a safe place for owls and the animals they hunt.

If you ever see an owl in your yard, stay quiet and give it space so it doesn't get scared away.

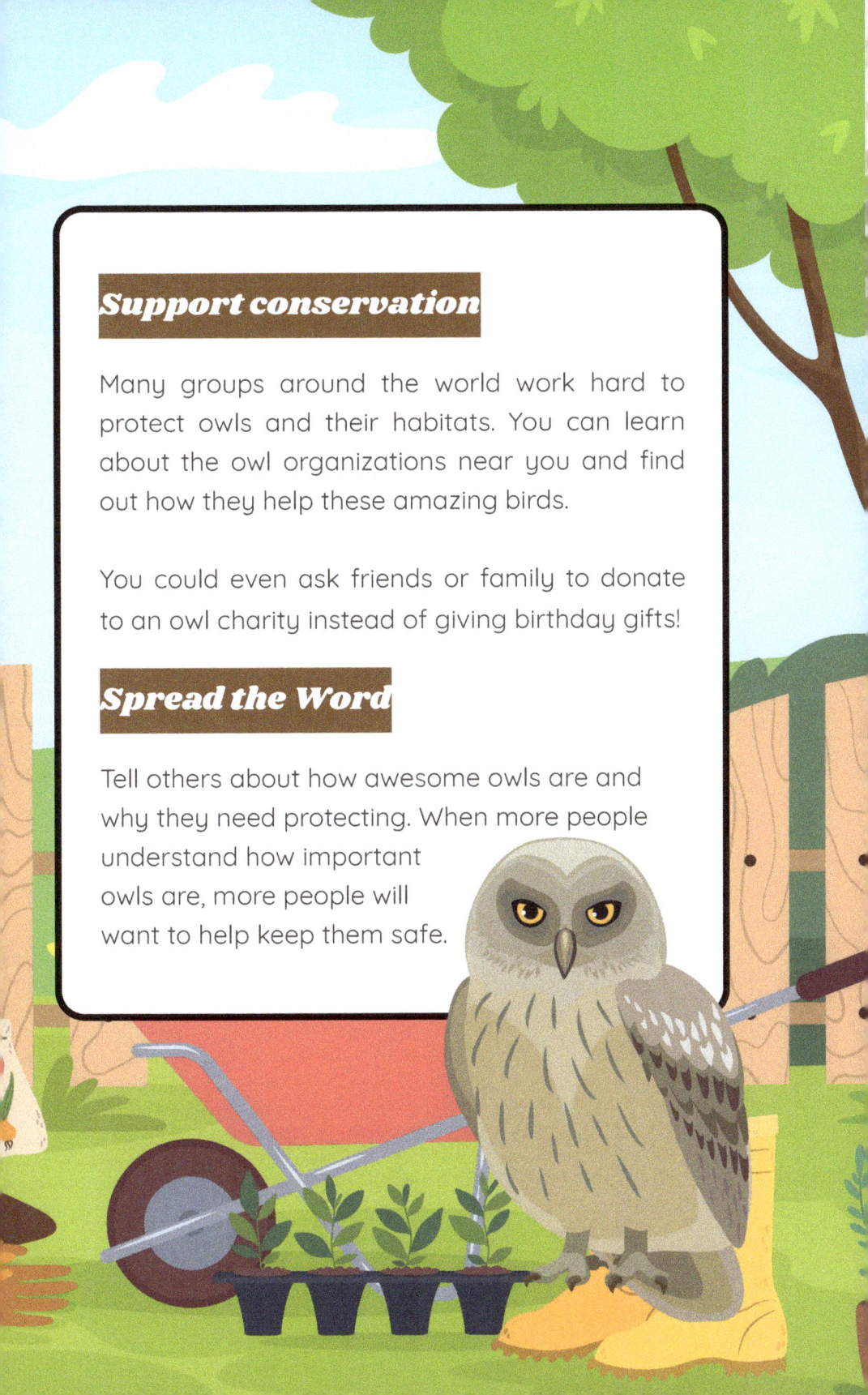

Support conservation

Many groups around the world work hard to protect owls and their habitats. You can learn about the owl organizations near you and find out how they help these amazing birds.

You could even ask friends or family to donate to an owl charity instead of giving birthday gifts!

Spread the Word

Tell others about how awesome owls are and why they need protecting. When more people understand how important owls are, more people will want to help keep them safe.

The Eurasian pygmy owl—Europe's smallest owl species.

OWLS & THE ECOSYSTEM

Owls play an important role in nature all around the world. As hunters, they help keep ecosystems healthy and balanced.

Without owls, some animals—like rodents and insects—could grow out of control. This can cause problems for plants, other animals, and even people. That's why owls are such an important part of the natural world!

Let's take a closer look at how owls help ecosystems stay healthy.

Natural Pest Control

Owls help control the numbers of rodents, insects, and other small animals. By hunting these creatures, owls stop their populations from growing too large.

This helps protect plants, crops, and forests from damage. It also benefits people, especially farmers, by naturally reducing pests—without the need for chemicals.

Keeping Nature in Balance

Owls are part of the food chain. They hunt some animals, but they can also be prey for larger predators.

By being both hunters and hunted, owls help keep a healthy balance between different animal populations. This

balance supports biodiversity and prevents any one species from becoming too common—or disappearing completely.

Indicator Species

Owls are known as **indicator species**. This means scientists can learn a lot about an ecosystem by studying owl populations.

If owl numbers begin to drop, it may be a sign that something is wrong—such as habitat loss, pollution, or fewer animals for them to eat. Healthy owl populations usually mean a healthy environment.

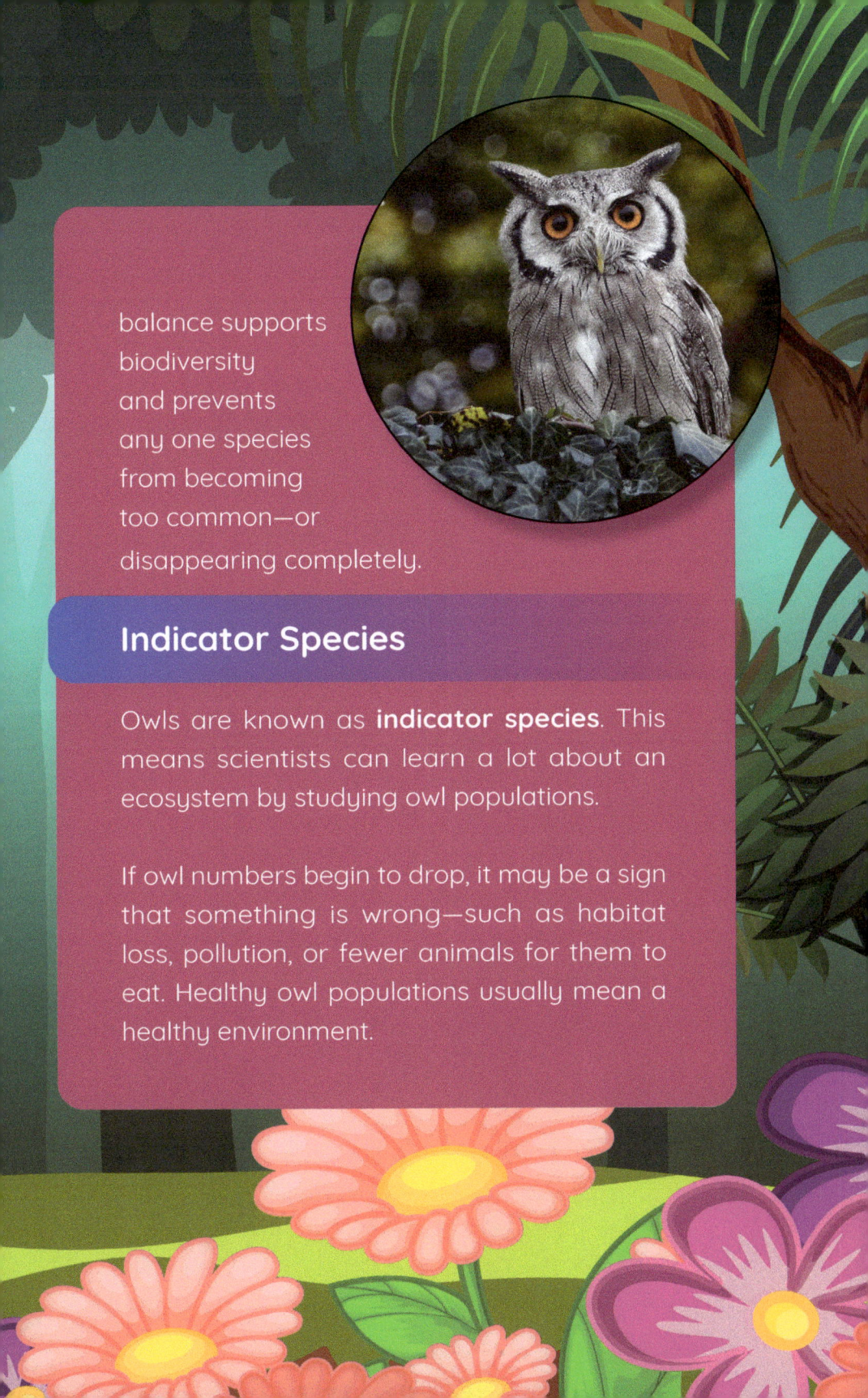

MORE OWL FUN FACTS

You've already learned so much about owls, but there's still more to discover! Prepare to dive into a treasure trove of fascinating and delightful fun facts about owls.

Afterwards, test yourself in the quiz!

There are more than 200 owl species worldwide.

Owls have three eyelids: one for blinking, one for sleeping, and one for cleaning their eyes!

Some owls, like the northern pygmy owl, have false "eye spots" on the back of their heads to confuse predators (**right**).

The elf owl is the smallest owl species, standing at just about 5 inches (12.7 cm) tall.

THE ULTIMATE OWL BOOK

The Eurasian eagle owl (**right**) is one of the largest owl species, with a wingspan of up to 6.5 feet (2 m).

• • •

The snowy owl can change the color of its feathers (by molting and growing new feathers with different markings) to match the changing seasons.

• • •

Owls can rotate their heads up to 270 degrees.

• • •

The tawny owl can live up to 20 years in the wild.

The barred owl (**left**) has dark "bars" on its chest, which give it its name.

• • •

The spectacled owl has white "glasses" around its eyes, resembling spectacles.

• • •

Some owls, like the long-eared owl, have tufts of feathers called "ear tufts" that are not related to their hearing.

• • •

The great grey owl is the tallest owl species, standing at about 27 inches (69 cm) tall.

Don't be fooled! The potoo owl (**right**) is not actually an owl. It gets its name from the distinctive 'pot-o-o-o-o-' call it makes!

• • •

Owls have zygodactyl feet, meaning they have two toes facing forward and two facing backward.

• • •

The burrowing owl is one of the few owl species that is active during the day.

• • •

The collared scops owl can change its body posture to resemble a branch.

Image: Charles J. Sharp

The ferruginous pygmy owl is known to mimic the sounds of other birds.

• • •

The Ural owl (**left**) is known for its aggressive behavior when defending its nest.

• • •

The Blakiston's fish owl is the largest owl species in Asia and is known for its fishing skills.

• • •

The barking owl gets its name from the dog-like barking sounds it makes!

The laughing owl, now extinct, was once found in New Zealand and was known for its eerie, human-like laugh.

• • •

The tawny frogmouth is not an owl. It belongs to a group of birds related to nightjars.

• • •

The northern spotted owl is endangered and lives in old-growth forests of the Pacific Northwest

• • •

The whiskered screech owl has whisker-like feathers around its beak.

The Madagascar red owl is extremely rare and was once thought to be extinct. It is known for its distinctive rusty-red colored feathers and is considered one of the rarest birds of prey in the world.

• • •

The Jamaican owl, also called the Jamaican screech owl, is found only in Jamaica.. It is mostly nocturnal and feeds on small mammals, birds, and insects.

• • •

The oriental bay owl has a distinctive heart-shaped facial disk.

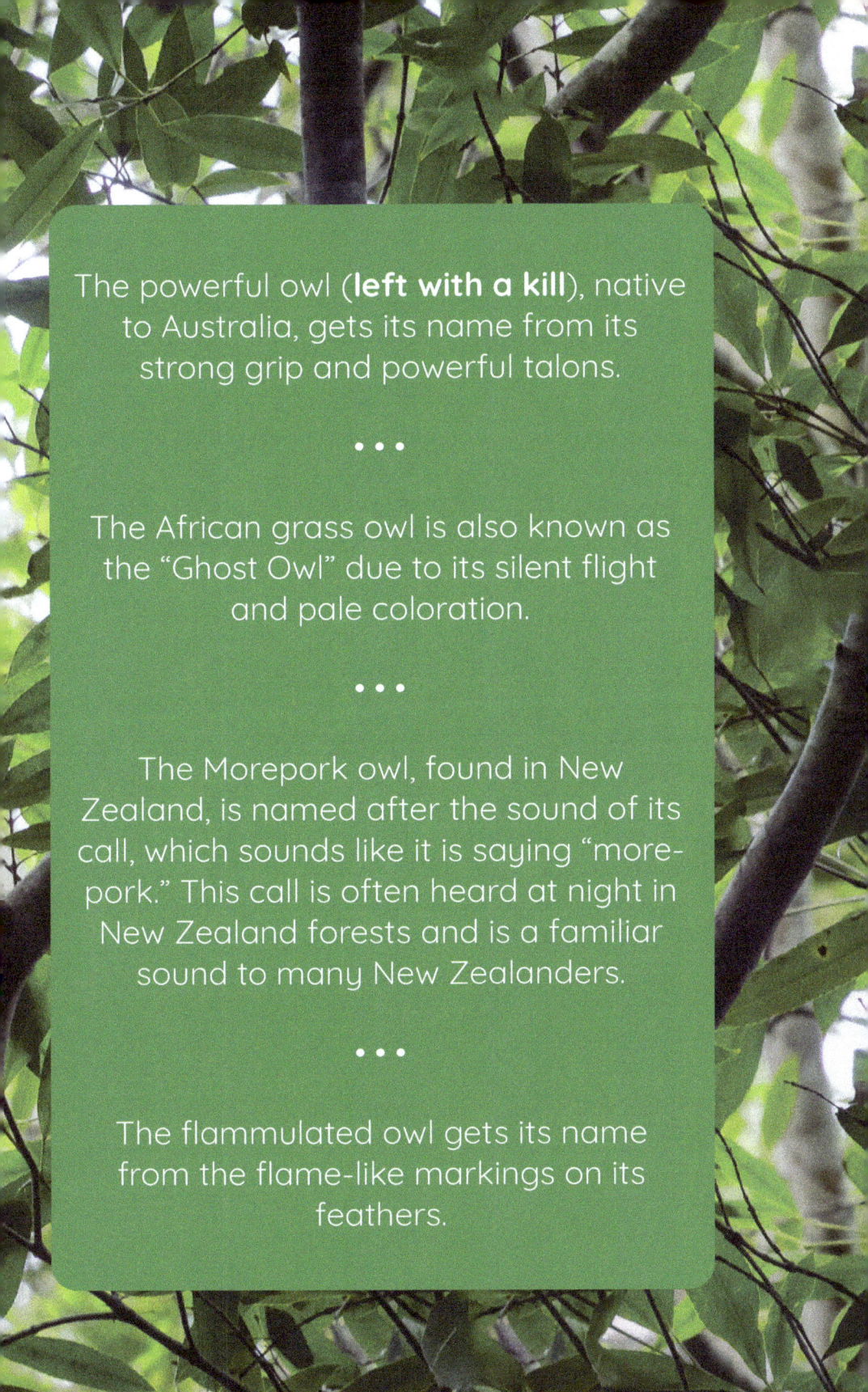

The powerful owl (**left with a kill**), native to Australia, gets its name from its strong grip and powerful talons.

• • •

The African grass owl is also known as the "Ghost Owl" due to its silent flight and pale coloration.

• • •

The Morepork owl, found in New Zealand, is named after the sound of its call, which sounds like it is saying "more-pork." This call is often heard at night in New Zealand forests and is a familiar sound to many New Zealanders.

• • •

The flammulated owl gets its name from the flame-like markings on its feathers.

The northern hawk owl is known for its hawk-like hunting behavior and appearance. Like other owls, it has special feathers that allow for quiet flight.

• • •

The Stygian owl is named after the river Styx from Greek mythology, which is associated with darkness and the underworld.

• • •

The sooty owl, found in Australia, gets its name from its dark, soot-like coloration. Unlike most owls that have yellow or orange eyes, the sooty owl has dark brown eyes, which may help it blend in better with its dark forested habitat.

Image: JJ Harrison

The rufous-legged owl is one of the few owl species found in South America's temperate rainforests.

• • •

The mottled owl has an intricate pattern of dark and light markings on its feathers, giving it a "mottled" appearance.

• • •

The forest owlet, native to India, was considered extinct until it was rediscovered in 1997.

• • •

The marsh owl (**left; owlets**), found in Africa, is one of the few owl species that prefer wetland habitats.

The Palau owl is a small owl species that is found only on the Palau Islands in the western Pacific Ocean.

• • •

The crested owl has a distinctive "crest" of feathers above its eyes.

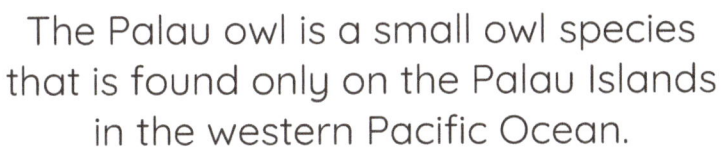

• • •

The Lesser Sunda Scops owl (**right**) is endemic to the Lesser Sunda Islands in Indonesia.

• • •

The great horned owl is sometimes called the "Tiger of the Sky" due to its powerful hunting abilities and distinctive markings.

The short-eared owl can be found on every continent except Australia and Antarctica.

Image: Nick Athanas

The pearl-spotted owlet has white "pearl" spots on its wings and back, giving it its name. Small owl species, such as this one, are often called 'owlets'.

• • •

The Cape eagle owl is native to South Africa and is known for its bright orange eyes.

• • •

The barn owl can be found on every continent except Antarctica, making it one of the most widespread owl species.

• • •

The Christmas Island hawk-owl is a rare species found only on Christmas Island, an Australian territory in the Indian Ocean.

The Owl Quiz

Were you paying attention?! Test your new owl knowledge!

1. What is the smallest owl species?

2. How many degrees can an owl rotate its head?

3. Which owl species has false "eye spots" on the back of its head?

4. What is the purpose of the heart-shaped face of some owl species?

5   Name one of the few owl species that is active during the day.

6   How do owls' ears help them pinpoint the location of sounds?

7   Which owl species is known for its fishing skills?

8   What is the primary reason for the decline in owl populations?

9   Name one of the few owl species that prefer wetland habitats.

10 How does the snowy owl change its appearance to match the changing seasons?

11 Which owl species is named after the river Styx from Greek mythology?

12 What does the term "zygodactyl feet" mean?

13 How do the tawny frogmouth and owls differ?

14 What is the purpose of providing artificial nest boxes for owls?

15 Which owl species is native to South Africa and has bright orange eyes?

16 Which owl species has a distinctive "crest" of feathers above its eyes?

17 Which owl species is sometimes called the "Tiger of the Sky"?

18 Name one of the threats that owls face due to climate change.

19 What is the primary method that owls use to communicate with each other?

20 In which stage of the life cycle do young owls learn to hunt and fly?

21 How do owls blend into their environment to avoid detection?

22 Which owl species was considered extinct until it was rediscovered in 1997?

ANSWERS

1. Elf owl
2. 270 degrees
3. Northern pygmy owl
4. To funnel sound to their ears
5. Burrowing owl
6. Their asymmetrically placed ears
7. Blakiston's fish owl
8. Habitat loss
9. Marsh Owl
10. By molting and growing new feathers with different markings
11. Stygian owl
12. They have two toes facing forward and two facing backward
13. The tawny frogmouth is a member of a family related to the nightjar, not an owl
14. To provide suitable nesting sites and help support owl populations

15. Cape eagle owl
16. Crested owl
17. Great horned owl
18. Changes in prey distribution or habitat loss
19. Vocalizations, such as hoots, screeches, and calls
20. Fledgling stage
21. Through their coloration and patterns on their feathers
22. Forest Owlet

Can you find all the words below in the word search puzzle on the right?

NOCTURNAL	**BARN OWL**	**TALONS**
PREDATOR	**HOOT**	**OWLET**
FEATHERS	**SNOWY**	**WISE**

Owls Word Search

T	D	S	A	C	B	G	S	P	Y	R	R
R	A	N	C	B	A	R	N	O	W	L	G
Q	S	N	O	W	Y	C	N	R	Z	D	F
S	C	V	E	C	Z	O	W	L	E	T	D
F	Q	W	G	F	T	B	V	X	P	Z	B
Q	E	D	M	J	G	U	D	A	R	E	V
T	T	A	L	O	N	S	R	C	E	F	C
R	E	Q	T	C	H	F	D	N	D	R	X
H	Q	Z	X	H	V	G	D	S	A	H	E
Q	O	H	G	S	E	B	V	E	T	L	R
V	Z	O	Z	V	Q	R	J	F	O	N	T
C	X	B	T	D	W	I	S	E	R	H	F

THE ULTIMATE OWL BOOK

SOLUTION

			N		B	A	R	N	O	W	L	
		S	N	O	W	Y						
				C		O	W	L	E	T		
	F				T				P			
		E				U			R			
		T	A	L	O	N	S	R		E		
			T				N	D				
H				H				A				
	O				E			T	L			
		O			R			O				
		T		W	I	S	E	R				

SOURCES

BirdLife International. (2021) 'IUCN Red List for Birds,' Available at: http://www.birdlife.org (Accessed: 24 April 2023).

Cornell Lab of Ornithology. (2021) 'All About Birds,' Available at: https://www.allaboutbirds.org/ (Accessed: 24 April 2023).

International Owl Center. (2021) 'Owl Information,' Available at: https://www.internationalowlcenter.org/ (Accessed: 24 April 2023).

Mikkola, H. (2012) 'Owls of the World: A Photographic Guide,' 2nd edn., London: Bloomsbury Publishing.

National Geographic Society. (2021) 'Owls: Overview, species, and habitats,' Available at: https://www.nationalgeographic.com/animals/birds/group/owls/ (Accessed: 24 April 2023).

Owl Research Institute. (2021) 'Owl Biology and Research,' Available at: https://www.owlresearchinstitute.org/ (Accessed: 24 April 2023).

Raptor Resource Project. (2021) 'Owl Facts and Information,' Available at: https://www.raptorresource.org/ (Accessed: 24 April 2023).

The Owl Pages. (2021) 'Information about Owls,' Available at: https://www.owlpages.com/ (Accessed: 24 April 2023).

World Owl Trust. (2021) 'Owl Conservation,' Available at: https://www.worldowltrust.org/ (Accessed: 24 April 2023).

"13 Fun Facts About Owls". 2015. Audubon. https://www.audubon.org/news/13-fun-facts-about-owls.

"Six Amazing Owl Facts To Give Two Hoots About | RSPB". 2023. The RSPB. https://www.rspb.org.uk/our-work/rspb-news/rspb-news-stories/six-amazing-owl-facts-to-give-two-hoots-about/.

Clifford, Garth. 2023. "17 Fascinating Owl Facts You Didn't Know (2023) - World Birds". World Birds. https://worldbirds.com/owl-facts/.

"Owl | Types, Species, & Facts". 2023. Encyclopedia Britannica. https://www.britannica.com/animal/owl.

You're a Hoot!

As our journey through the world of owls comes to an end, we hope you've enjoyed learning about these fascinating birds as much as we enjoyed sharing their story with you.

Your feedback means a lot to us, so we kindly ask you to **leave a review** on the platform where you purchased the book.

Your thoughts and experiences will help other readers discover the captivating world of owls and encourage us to continue creating engaging and educational content for all.

Thank you for your support!

ALSO BY JENNY KELLETT

 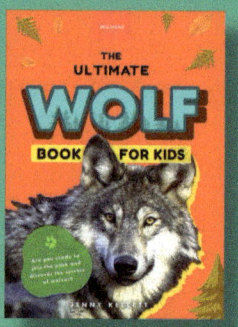 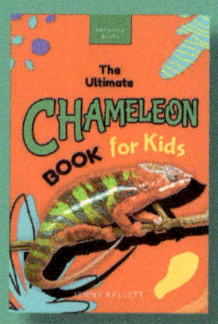

... and more!

Available at
www.bellanovabooks.com
and all major online bookstores.

www.ingramcontent.com/pod-product-compliance
Lightning Source LLC
LaVergne TN
LVHW050842080526
838202LV00009B/317